World of Wonders

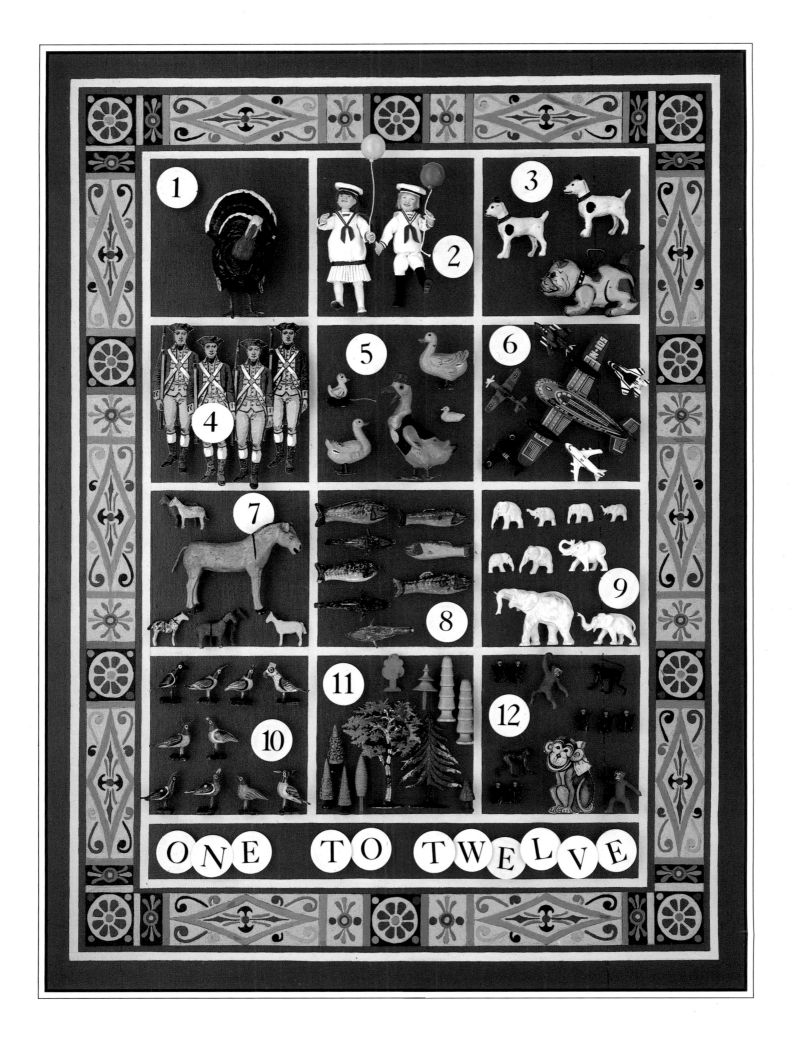

World of Wonders

A Trip Through Numbers

Photographs by Starr Ockenga

Poem and Painted Backgrounds
by Eileen Doolittle

Houghton Mifflin Company · Boston

A FLOYD YEAROUT BOOK

To the memory of Audrey Williamson Ockenga,
friend to many children
And to our own children Kathy, Chip, and Robin

Also by Starr Ockenga and Eileen Doolittle
The Ark in the Attic

Other books by Starr Ockenga
Mirror after Mirror
Dressup: Playacts and Fantasies of Childhood

A FLOYD YEAROUT BOOK
Photographs copyright © 1988 by Starr Ockenga · Text copyright © 1988 by Eileen Doolittle
All rights reserved. For information about permission to reproduce selections from this book, write to:
Permissions, Houghton Mifflin Company, 2 Park Street, Boston, Massachusetts 02108

Library of Congress Cataloging-in-Publication Data

Ockenga, Starr.
World of wonders.

"A Floyd Yearout book." Bibliography: p. 48
Summary: A counting book with detailed photographs for each number from one to twelve,
depicting a multitude of subjects commonly associated with each number.
1. Counting — Juvenile literature. 2. Number concept — Juvenile literature.
[1. Counting. 2. Number concept] I. Doolittle, Eileen. II. Title.
QA113.028 1988   513'.2 [E]   88-9032   ISBN 0-395-48726-9

X 10 9 8 7 6 5 4 3 2 1

PRINTED IN ITALY

Photographer's Note

The child is eternal, and so are toys and tears and laughter.
When the house is put in order by strange men, when the clothes that were worn
and the tools that were used are put away, there will be found
an upper room full of toys. These remain.

The Toy Shop, MARGARITA SPALDING GERRY

COUNTING IS PART OF COLLECTING. WHEN ONE LOVES CLOWNS, tin trains, or wooden ark animals, the accumulating instinct has few bounds. No one who becomes enamored of a certain kind of object is satisfied to own just one. This book is about that process of hunting and adding. We joined our own collections, borrowed from friends, and counted what we had assembled. Of course, over those months we also bought more. "We only need one more frog, two more airplanes, three more beaded evening bags . . ." Making this book gave us license to do what we like best: collect.

Quickly, too, with a partner in such a search, the process became a game. Many of the assembled objects naturally fell under a particular number, just by their association with that number: one-armed bandit, twins, three blind mice, seven dwarfs, twelve months of the year. We also found ourselves playing with the numbers – recalling references to children's literature, lines from songs, film and play titles, or vernacular expressions, like "Three Billy Goats Gruff," "Five-Finger Exercise," "behind the eight ball," and all "Twelve Days of Christmas." We invite you to discover those connections and to invent new ones. Other objects are included just because we are partial to them. Yet, gathered together, they seemed to suggest a theme or mood for the photograph – "Once in a Blue Moon," "Tea for Two," "Three-Ring Circus"; those became our working titles, and another level of our game. (A key to the photographs is provided at the back of the book.)

For us, these small treasures are tangible links to the sweet, distant moments of our own childhoods. Toys are, we fancy, what help keep us young. In the hands of our small friends, these dolls, blocks, and soldiers are tools for building what will become their memories in the future.

STARR OCKENGA

1 One I

The ringmaster calls from far away.
"Come one, come all," he seems to say.
"There is a wondrous world around us
And countless creatures who'll astound us."

To enter this enchanted space
We need a magic talisman.
A heart that's brave could be the thing,
An elf or key or unicorn;
Or winged folk bestowing grace
Could guide us to this strange new place.

Find a penny head-side up.
It's thought to bring one great good luck.
Hold it tight, and close your eyes —
There's bound to be a big surprise.

1

2 Two II

We've landed in the mezzanine,
Watching dancers float in sight.
Two marionettes do pirouettes,
While sipping cups of tea.

The Tweedle brothers, Dum and Dee,
Can't help us in our flight.
They always act contrariwise –
They fuss and feud and fight.

3 Three III

(Turn the page, please.)

3 Three wishes bring a three-ring circus,

With ghosts and goats and bears on chairs.

4 Four IV

Suddenly the world's before us,
And four-leaf clovers pay our fares.
Let's pick a place that's glamorous.
We can choose to travel anywhere!

4

5

5 Five V

Parading down Fifth Avenue
Is a fashionable thing to do.
The buildings here are straight and tall,
And players play at basketball.
Count golden rings without delay,
And mystically we're on our way.

6 Six VI

(Turn the page, please.)

6   Six geese do feats of derring-do,

And beasts have feasts of birthday cakes.

6

7 Seven VII

Too soon we're whisked to some place new
By magic-feathered swans in queue.
Seven sledders slide on flakes,
And skaters glide on icy lakes,
While snowmen pose with Santa Claus.
It's much too cold for us to pause.

8

8 Eight VIII

Eight lily pads and eight reindeer.
Just what can be enchanted here?
Were the winged folk once butterflies?
Is a toad a prince in frog disguise?

9 Nine IX

(Turn the page, please.)

9   Nine planets now are on the rise.

We'll have no time to itemize.

10 Ten X

We're plunging in the briny deep,
Past fish and ships, ten dimes and signs;
Pipers, sailors, and chicks that peep.
Seek spellbound stones that we can keep
To help us on our merry way,
Unless, of course, you'd like to stay.

1 2 3 4 5 6 7 8 9 10

10

11 Eleven XI

A ballroom whirls and twirls around us.
Bewitching perfume fills the air.
Eleven minstrels' tunes surround us.
Can we leave without fanfare?

12 Twelve XII

(Turn the page, please.)

12   At twelve we reach the monkeys' lair.

It's clear that we've been everywhere.

The ringmaster calls from far away.
"Come one, come all," he seems to say
"Wake up, get ready without delay.
The circus is here, it's a holiday!"

Was this a dream we happened to share?
Is the bear on the bed the bear in the chair?
Was Vincent van Gogh in a one-man show?
What do you think? Will we ever know?

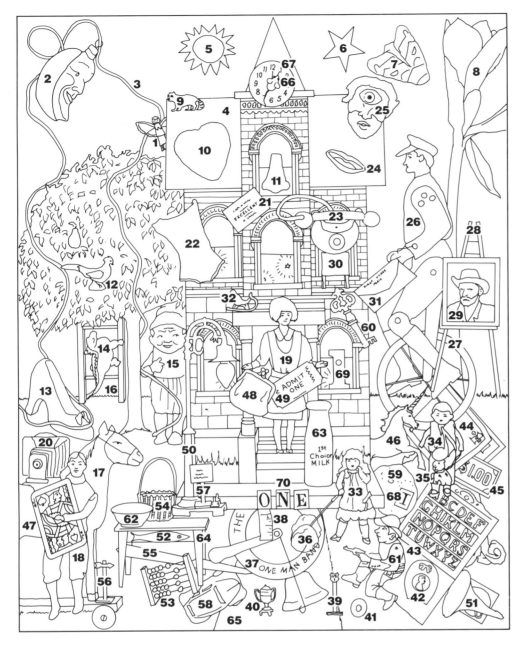

25. cyclops, one-eyed giant
26. unicyclist
27. unicycle
28. easel
29. painting, one-man show
30. nightstand
31. letter, first-class mail
32. sleigh, "In a one-horse open sleigh" (from a song)
33. girl
34. boy, "Johnny One Note" (song)
35. dog
36. butterfly net
37. one-man band
38. inch
39. U.S. 1
40. trophy, first-prize
41. record, *One for the Record* (book)
42. lucky penny
43. horn book, a children's primer
44. dollar, "One for the Money" (nursery rhyme)
45. $1.00 tag
46. unicorn
47. one-eyed jack
48. purse
49. ticket, "Admit One"
50. lamp post
51. gramophone with monaural sound
52. fish; "One Fish, Two Fish" (nursery rhyme)
53. abacus
54. basket, "One Basket" (short story)
55. file, single file
56. One Way
57. One Hour Parking
58. car, "one for the road"
59. potato; "One potato, two potato" (nursery rhyme)
60. key
61. bandit, one-armed bandit
62. bowl
63. bottle
64. table; "My father, he left me
Just as he was able,
One bowl, one bottle, one table."
(from a nursery rhyme)
65. path
66. mouse
67. one o'clock, "The mouse ran up the clock" (nursery rhyme)
68. roman numeral
69. arabic numeral; a hole in one (golf)
70. O N E, spelled out

---

1 One I
Once in a Blue Moon

1. winged folk
2. moon, "once in a blue moon"
3. string, first string (sports)
4. house, single-family dwelling
5. sun
6. star; "Star light, star bright,
First star I see tonight" (from a nursery rhyme)
7. moth
8. amaryllis
9. raccoon, *One Raccoon Dancing in the Moon* (book)
10. heart, *One from the Heart* (movie)

11. nose
12. a partridge in a pear tree (from the song, "The Twelve Days of Christmas")
13. Cinderella's glass slipper
14. dragon, *One Dragon Too Many* (book)
15. guardian elf
16. ladder
17. horse, "one-horse town"
18. father
19. mother
20. camera with monocular vision
21. merit
22. one-piece bathing suit
23. telephone
24. mouth

2 Two II
"Tea for Two"

1. puppets
2. winged folk
3. pictures
4. pair of pears
5. tennis partners (doubles)
6. sets of grandparents, one set dancing to "It Takes Two to Tango," (song)
7. chess kings
8. chess queens
9. score cards counting 1, 2
10. pairs of socks
11. ballerinas in tutus
12. trained dogs
13. pair of candlesticks
14. bicycles
15. bicyclists
16. pairs of gloves
17. cups; "Tea for Two" (song)
18. saucers
19. tea bags
20. cinnamon sticks
21. pairs of glasses
22. pairs of dice
23. eyes
24. two-dollar bills, American and Canadian
25. candy bells
26. tassels
27. pairs of scissors
28. chopsticks
29. turtle doves ("The Twelve Days of Christmas")
30. hands
31. fencing foils
32. tacks
33. pairs of shoes
34. sets of twins, infants and Tweedledum and Tweedledee
35. binoculars
36. dolphins
37. pfennigs, German coins
38. tulips
39. couples
40. two o'clock
41. roman numeral
42. arabic numeral
43. T W O, spelled out

3 Three III
Three-Ring Circus

1. circus rings
2. faces, *Three Faces of Eve* (movie)
3. winged folk
4. ghosts, "Three Little Ghostesses" (nursery rhyme)
5. French hens ("The Twelve Days of Christmas")
6. "Three Green Twigs" (fairy tale)
7. wishbones
8. cats, "Three Little Kittens" (nursery rhyme)
9. parasols
10. dolls, "The Three Sisters" (play)
11. sheets, "three sheets to the wind"
12. clothespins
13. 3 Musketeers bars
14. tricolor flags
15. wise men
16. "Three Golden Hairs" (fairy tale)
17. ringmasters
18. "Three Feathers" (fairy tale)
19. dogs, "Three young dogs with curling tails" (from a nursery rhyme)
20. Betty Boop buttons
21. clowns
22. trio
23. triplets
24. "Three Cows" (nursery rhyme)
25. "The Three Magic Oranges" (fairy tale)

26. goats, "The Three Billy Goats Gruff" (fairy tale)
27. "Three bags full" (from a nursery rhyme)
28. Graces: Faith, Hope, and Charity
29. 3-D glasses
30. "Three Foxes" (fairy tale)
31. anemones
32. ranunculus
33. "The Three Little Pigs" (fairy tale)
34. gingerbread men
35. "Three men in a tub,
    A butcher, a baker, a candlestick maker"(from a nursery rhyme)
36. men, "Three on a match"
37. chairs
38. "The Three Bears" (fairy tale)
39. "Three Blind Mice" (nursery rhyme)
40. dark glasses
41. canes
42. acrobats
43. monkeys, "hear no evil, see no evil, speak no evil"
44. Three-Legged Race ribbon
45. three-sided figure, triangle
46. coins
47. ducklings
48. three o'clock
49. Lotto chips, counting 1, 2, 3
50. roman numeral
51. arabic numeral
52. T H R E E, spelled out

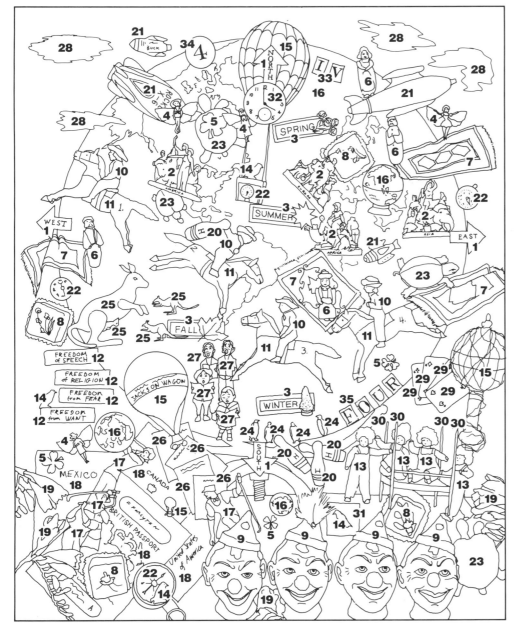

Four Corners of the Earth

1. directions: north, south, east, west
2. corners of the earth: Asia, Africa, Europe, America
3. seasons of the year: spring, summer, fall, winter
4. winged folk
5. four-leaf clovers, "One leaf for fame,
   One leaf for wealth,
   One for a faithful lover,
   And one leaf to bring glorious health
   Are all in a four-leaf clover." (nursery rhyme)
6. sugar people
7. magic carpets
8. petits fours
9. clowns, in the foreground, with forelocks on big foreheads
10. cowboys
11. horses, quadrupeds, four-footed animals, counting 1, 2, 3, 4
12. freedoms: of speech, of religion, from fear, from want
13. quadruplets
14. calling birds ("The Twelve Days of Christmas")
15. hot-air balloons
16. globes
17. golfing foursome shouting "Fore!"
18. passports
19. freesia
20. 4-H clubs
21. rocket ships
22. compasses
23. turtles
24. penguins
25. kangaroos
26. newspapers, "the fourth estate"
27. barbershop quartet
28. cotton clouds
29. cards of four suits: diamonds, clubs, spades, hearts
30. posts on a four-poster bed
31. four-sided figure, square, quadrangle
32. four o'clock
33. roman numeral
34. arabic numeral
35. F O U R, (a four-letter word) spelled out

5 Five V
"On the Avenue, Fifth Avenue"

1. five-pointed stars
2. streamers
3. senses: hearing, taste, touch, smell, sight
4. Bill Dings
5. winged folk
6. appliances: coffee maker, mixer, fan, refrigerator, vacuum cleaner
7. racing cars, Indianapolis 500
8. quintuplets, *Five Little Rich Girls* (book)
9. Easter bonnets
10. Easter baskets with Easter bunnies
11. golden rings ("The Twelve Days of Christmas")
12. five-story houses
13. painted buildings
14. lobsters
15. nickels
16. 5 Cents signs
17. peppers, *Five Little Peppers and How They Grew* (book)
18. wheels, "fifth wheel"
19. puzzle pieces, *Five Easy Pieces* (movie)
20. basketball players—a team
21. basketballs
22. five fingers, *Five Finger Exercise* (play)
23. alligators
24. piglets: "This little piggy went to market" (from a nursery rhyme)
25. columns, "fifth column"
26. brick blocks
27. red building blocks
28. tin window blocks
29. Christmas cottages
30. counting blocks, 1, 2, 3, 4, 5
31. gladiolus blossoms
32. five-dollar bill
33. five-sided figure, pentagon
34. 55 speed limit
35. 5th Avenue, "On the avenue, Fifth Avenue" (from a song)
36. five o'clock
37. roman numeral
38. arabic numeral
39. F I V E, spelled out, "high five"

6 Six VI
"Now We Are Six"

1. zoo buildings
2. candles
3. birthday cakes
4. streamers
5. elephants, *Now We Are Six* (book)
6. winged folk
7. lions
8. polar bears
9. camels
10. zebras
11. giraffes
12. geese-a-laying ("The Twelve Days of Christmas")
13. masks
14. presents
15. hats
16. balloons

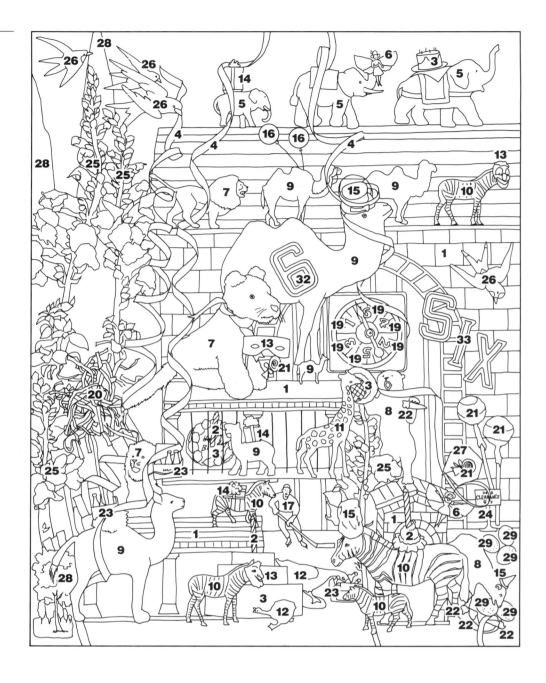

17. hockey players—a team
18. horse game discs, counting 1, 2, 3, 4, 5, 6
19. game spinner divided into sections 1 to 6
20. noisemakers
21. lollipops
22. ice cream cones
23. six-packs of Coca-Cola
24. Head Clearance 6 Feet
25. snapdragons
26. "bluebirds of happiness"
27. six-sided figure, hexagon
28. trees
29. eggs, one-half dozen
30. six o'clock
31. roman numeral
32. arabic numeral
33. S I X, spelled out

6

7 Seven VII
Seventh Heaven

1. angels, "seventh heaven"
2. sledders
3. days of the week: Monday, Tuesday, Wednesday, Thursday, Friday, Saturday, Sunday
4. knights with lances
5. Deadly Sins: pride, covetousness, lust, anger, gluttony, envy, sloth
6. swans-a-swimming ("The Twelve Days of Christmas")
7. winged folk
8. 7-Up bottle caps
9. snowmen
10. Santas
11. cees
12. skaters
13. dwarfs
14. poinsettia
15. fir trees
16. brooms
17. candy canes
18. snowflakes
19. silver bells
20. rainbow, seven colors: red, orange, yellow, green, blue, indigo, violet
21. counting 1, 2, 3, 4, 5, 6, 7
22. seven o'clock
23. roman numeral
24. arabic numeral
25. S E V E N, spelled out

8 Eight VIII
"Dinner at Eight"

1. frogs
2. butterflies
3. bugs
4. golden balls
5. eight tiny reindeer (from "The Night Before Christmas," a poem)
6. maids-a-milking ("The Twelve Days of Christmas")
7. silk water lilies
8. winged folk
9. lily pads
10. plates, *Dinner at Eight* (play)
11. eight ball, "behind the eight ball"
12. eight-sided figure, octagon
13. notes, an octave
14. Lotto chips, counting 1, 2, 3, 4, 5, 6, 7, 8
15. eight o'clock
16. roman numeral
17. arabic numeral
18. E I G H T, spelled out

9 Nine IX
"Engine, Engine, Number Nine"

1. trains, "Engine, Engine, Number
   Nine" (nursery rhyme)
2. tracks
3. cars
4. planets: Mercury, Venus, Earth,
   Mars, Jupiter, Saturn, Uranus,
   Neptune, Pluto
5. policemen
6. trucks
7. nests
8. birds
9. winged folk
10. dogs
11. drummers drumming ("The Twelve
    Days of Christmas")
12. rocks

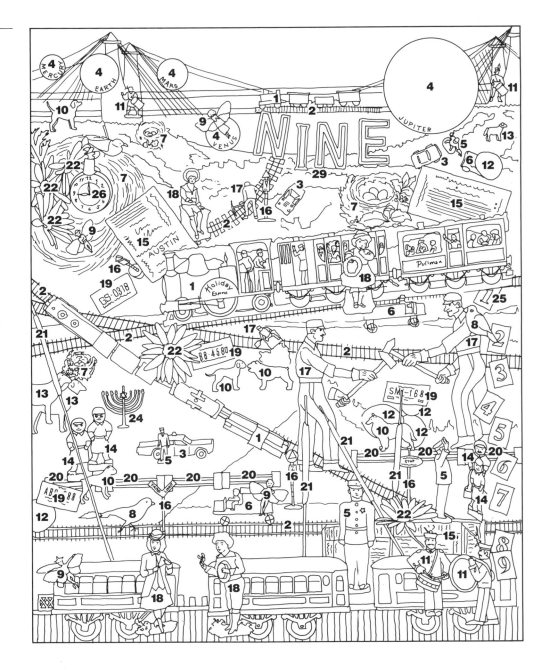

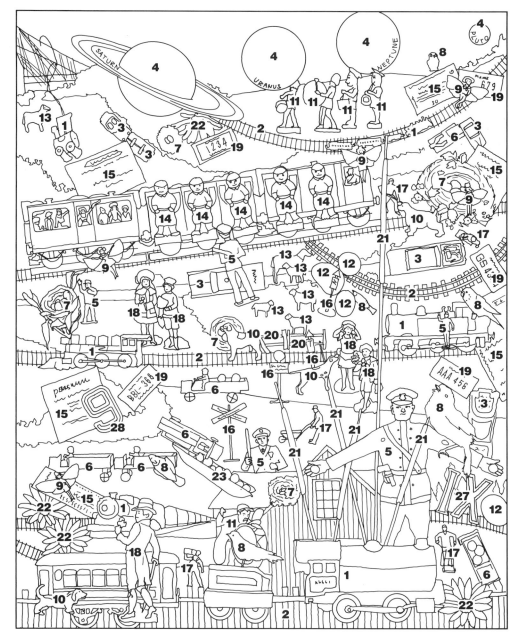

13. sheep
14. baseball players—a team
15. train tickets
16. railroad signs
17. workmen
18. children "dressed to the nines"
19. license plates
20. fence sections
21. cat-o'-nine-tails
22. daisies
23. peas in a pod ("When nine are found, the next man through the door will be your husband," an old wives tale)
24. nine-armed candelabrum, Menorah
25. counting 1, 2, 3, 4, 5, 6, 7, 8, 9
26. nine o'clock
27. roman numeral
28. arabic numeral
29. N I N E, spelled out

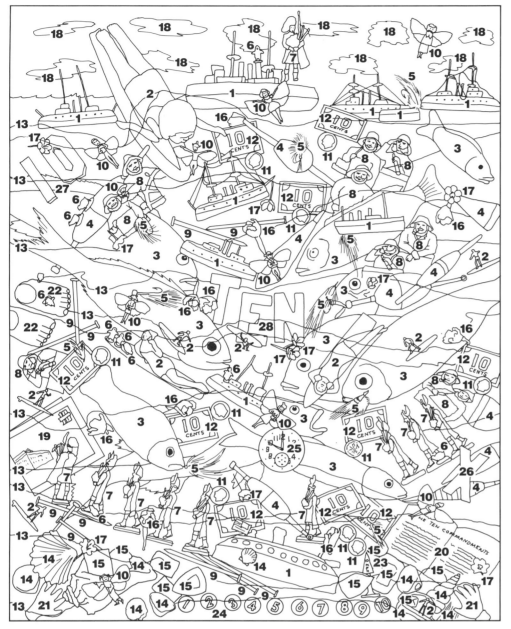

10 Ten X
Hang Ten

1. boats
2. surfers on surfboards, "hang ten"
3. fish
4. bobbers
5. lures
6. "Ten Chickens" (nursery rhyme)
7. pipers piping ("The Twelve Days of Christmas")
8. mariners
9. ten-penny nails
10. winged folk
11. dimes
12. 10 Cents signs
13. waves
14. shells
15. gem stones
16. delphinium blossoms
17. allium blossoms
18. cotton clouds
19. ten dollars
20. Ten Commandments
21. fingers: "I have ten little fingers, And they all belong to me." (poem)
22. toes
23. 10 M.P.H.
24. counting 1, 2, 3, 4, 5, 6, 7, 8, 9, 10
25. ten o'clock
26. roman numeral
27. arabic numeral
28. T E N, spelled out

11 Eleven XI
"Eleven Ladies Dancing"

1. ladies dancing ("The Twelve Days of Christmas")
2. animal musicians
3. football players—a team
4. soccer players—a team
5. fans
6. candy hearts, "elevenses"
7. crystalized violets
8. evening bags
9. perfume bottles
10. potted palms
11. winged folk
12. dance programs
13. dance pencils
14. roses
15. counting 1, 2, 3, 4, 5, 6, 7, 8, 9, 10, 11
16. eleven o'clock
17. roman numeral
18. arabic numeral
19. E L E V E N, spelled out

12 Twelve XII
"High Noon"

1. monkeys
2. Christmas balls
3. lords-a-leaping ("The Twelve Days of Christmas")
4. tritomas
5. lilies of the valley
6. quail eggs, *Cheaper by the Dozen* (book)
7. bananas
8. asparagus
9. twelve checkers to a side
10. forks
11. months of the year
12. winged folk

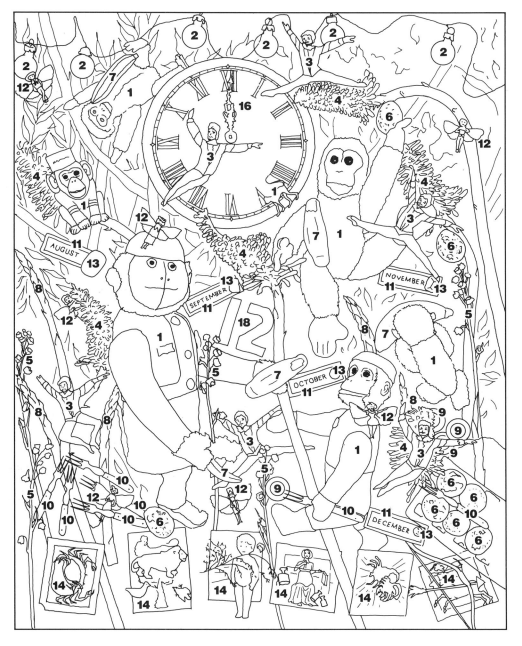

13. birthstones: January, garnet; February, amethyst; March, bloodstone; April, diamond; May, emerald; June, pearl; July, ruby; August, moonstone; September, sapphire; October, opal; November, topaz; December, turquoise

14. signs of the zodiac: Capricorn, a mountain goat; Aquarius, the water bearer; Pisces, the fish; Aries, the ram; Taurus, the bull; Gemini, the twins; Cancer, the crab; Leo, the lion; Virgo, the virgin with a sheaf of wheat; Scorpio, the scorpion; Sagittarius, the centaur with bow and arrow

15. ruler, counting 1, 2, 3, 4, 5, 6, 7, 8, 9, 10, 11, 12

16. twelve o'clock, *High Noon* (movie)

17. roman numeral

18. arabic numeral

19. T W E L V E, spelled out

Acknowledgments

WE ARE GRATEFUL to The Children's Museum of Indianapolis, especially to Peter V. Sterling, Executive Director, and Paul K. Richard, Deputy Director of Museum Programs, for their support of the accompanying exhibition; to Judi Ryan for her coordination and planning of the project, and Joy Johnson Crenshaw for her exhibition design.

We thank Roberta Batt, Molly Blayney, Mac Brown, Judith Castle, Peter Ciavarella, Ortega De Kauffman, Mary Donaldson, Agnes Doody, Ginnie and Ray Flemming, Barbara Gentiluomo, Marion Harris, Eileen and Hugh Kavanagh, Kyle Kloppe, Inger Kynaston, Ellen Liman, Christopher Mark, Mary Martin, Justine Maxon, Mystic Travel, Cathy Parker, Chip Parker, Elaine Skinner, Nicky Trench, Bill Wright, and Gery and Floyd Yearout, who helped in our search for small objects and who opened their private collections to us; Diane Smoler for creating the lovely ballerina in a tutu and the dancing ladies; Bill Wright for his technical assistance and good humor through all the photographing sessions; Susan Marsh for her book design that so enhances our work; Mary Reilly for the charm and delicacy of her schematic drawings; Floyd Yearout for his continued guidance, his professional expertise, and his nurturing of our efforts; and Walter Lorraine at Houghton Mifflin Company for his enthusiasm to publish *World of Wonders*.

Bibliography

Allison, Christine. *I'll Tell You a Story, I'll Sing You a Song*. New York: Delacorte Press, 1987.

Baring-Gould, William S. and Cecil. *The Annotated Mother Goose*. New York: Branhall House/Clarkson Potter, 1962.

Gerry, Margarita Spalding. *The Toy Shop, A Romantic Story of Lincoln the Man*. New York and London: Harper and Brothers, 1908.

Lang, Andrew. *The Green Fairy Book*. New York: Viking Press, 1969.

Lang, Andrew. *The Red Fairy Book*. New York: McKay Publishers, 1948.

Mitchell, Susanne. *The Larousse Book of Nursery Rhymes*. New York: Larousse and Company, 1984.

Rogers, James. *The Dictionary of Cliches*. New York: Ballantine Books, 1985.

Untermeyer, Louis. *Rainbow in the Sky*. New York: Harcourt Brace Jovanovich, 1963.

DESIGNED BY SUSAN MARSH

SCHEMATICS DRAWN BY MARY REILLY

TYPE SET IN GALLIARD BY MONOTYPE COMPOSITION COMPANY

PRODUCTION COORDINATED BY TRILOGY · PRINTED BY MAZZUCCHELLI · MILAN · ITALY